The Path To Loving Yourself:
You ARE a big deal!

Dr. Jessica Kerzner, Psy.D.

This book is dedicated to all the patients who have suffered but worked tirelessly to overcome the darkness within and find the light. The light is where we feel the love and this book is dedicated to all who strive to let the light in.

CONTENTS

ACKNOWLEDGMENTS:

I would like to thank numerous people for helping me take this project from a thought to a tangible product. First, I would like to thank my wonderful husband for being my rock and shoulder through long nights and endless mind sessions. My two boys for the endless laughter and joy they bring and for allowing their mother time to give to others.

I would also like to thank my mother for always reminding me that there is a way for any dream to become a reality and for helping me on this path in so many ways. My dad for never letting me settle on an idea without a challenge for it to be the best it can be. To Erin Courtney and Jennifer Bunch, thank you for a solid start on the path to helping others heal. You both provided a strong clinical foundation and an example of passion for healing.

A big thank you to my entire family and close friends. You all have been great delivering encouragement, insight, and true motivation for me during this process. I love each and every one of you.

To all, forever thankful.

Jessica Kerzner

1
THE PATH TO LOVING YOURSELF

Love is defined as an intense or deep feeling of affection towards a person or thing. We use the word love often and understand it when it relates to loving our parents, children, siblings, friends, and even coworkers. Often the struggle comes with loving ourselves. We look in a mirror and we don't look at ourselves with that same, deep affection. We are there looking, but we feel and see the past failures we have had, the past injuries others have given us, and all-out flaws we magnify each day.

The Path to Loving Yourself was brought to life when I realized that this was not only a path I had to walk down, but many people are struggling to find it. I see patients daily who their main struggle is they do not love themselves. They come into my office and the presenting problem is never "I don't love myself." It is often depression, anxiety, a bad relationship, behavior problems, addiction, etc. The root of a lot of them, that are not primarily biological in etiology, is that they don't love themselves. I can relate. There was a time I did not love myself and the path to loving myself was not highlighted on the web or in a book.

I had to figure out how to get there. So this book's goal is not to get raving reviews for being written perfectly. I have written it to speak to the reader and hopefully hold your attention. It is here to attempt to make a difference. I understand the pain and emptiness that is associated with not loving yourself and I witness it daily with my patients. It's a pain that can be removed over time if you make the choice to begin on this path. The path is curvy and has many steps but it is worth it.

I have a speech that I present related to this topic that shares my story of when I realized I was not loving myself. Let's start there. We are starting this road to loving yourself together. See you at the end. Dr. K.

You Are A Big Deal Speech

Dr. Jessica Kerzner

(Staring in the MIRROR!!) Are you doing what Michael Jackson says? Are you (singing)"Talking to the man in the mirror?" Oh wait. He says starting with the man in the mirror!! I always sing my own version of songs. Do you ever do that?? (LOL)

Well, for today we're going to pretend that he sings my version. (LOL). Sooooo - *(singing)* I'm Talking to the man in the mirror. Are you (*singing*) "asking him to change his ways?"

Do you remember junior high school? I do. Man, that was a time. I was about average height and build, but when I looked in the mirror all I saw was BAD HAIR. I had a ponytail back here and a bang I gelled down the side of my face here. Yeah. My mom stopped styling my hair so GEL became my friend. THANKS MOM!! (LOL)

I worked hard on that slick, gelled down, bang in the mirror. By the end of the day it stuck straight out, (*hold out hand*) like so, and resembled a TRIANGLE!!! You laugh but this is a true story. (LOL) I had bangs out to here, 1 pimple. Well, maybe... You know, everyone had 1 pimple. Sooo, maybe I had more. Like 5...6...7... Let's just say I had lots of acne.

My clothes resembled the bright side of a Crayola box! I'm talking: forest green pants, yellow shirt, and apple red sneakers. Again, THANKS MOM. (LOL)

She actually allowed me to pick out my own clothes because at that age of COURSE I knew EVERYTHING!! (LOL - *shake head in shame*)

OK, now I'm starting to think something may have been wrong with my mom, (*smile*) but she let me pick - and I picked forest green, apple red and yellow.

My ensemble was not complete though! Not without - an OVERSIZED T-shirt! Now, you may say "that's not a color." The color.
(*Shake head, shift to a more serious tone*)

The color didn't matter. It just had to be **massively** large on me. Why? Because I wanted to hide. Of course none of you know about wanting to hide because you all are, or were, supermodels.
(*pause*)

I knew. I didn't want to be noticed. I wanted to be invisible and guess what? BIG T-shirt. (*snap fingers*) Poof - I was hidden!!

I blended in, and that's what I wanted. Because I didn't think I was a big deal. Because when I was in the mirror, I stared at it. I didn't talk to the girl in the mirror. I wanted her to just make it day by day. I just wanted to BE!

You guys know what it is to just BE! Life comes and goes while you do your job or your chores. You see your family and your friends, but nothing stands out. Not them. Not you. (*pause, nod head*) That's what I wanted. That was safe to me.

I avoided photographs and I dreaded the spotlight. Wait. I'm up here. I'm not an imposter. I'm not pretending. So - what happened!!!??!! Somehow I stopped staring in the mirror and I started - what did Michael Jackson sing? "Talking to the man in the mirror."

I went to a small high school. I'm talking, 86 people in my entire class and 240 people in the entire school SMALL. You want to talk about trying to be invisible? Yeah, it didn't go so well for me there. Classes of 5 people. That oversized T-shirt lost it power! (LOL)

There was a teacher in my high school. Her name was Mrs. Preslar. She was a pretty lady. Smart, confident, but a normal amount of insecurity, right? Like, you know, she would talk to her coworkers, my other teachers, about her hair and then ask us KNOW IT ALL students how her hair looked when she changed it. That was not a good idea! (LOL)

One time she got a haircut and asked a few teachers about it before class began. They sang praises about it. Later she asked me about it and I said, "Honestly I think it's not right for your head!" Her response was "Gee, thanks Jessica!" Now. Why did she ask me? She was crushed and I'm sitting there thinking nothing looked good enough on me. How could I think anything would look good on anyone else? Remember I wanted to just BE!! But she, (*pause*) she was great and I knew it. I didn't know about that haircut - but I knew she was great!

She was a motivator, Mrs. Preslar. Every day she would tell me "Great job!" I would get to class and she would complement my hair. Must have been on days I didn't gel my forehead going after that bang. (LOL)

But one day she said something I'll never forget. I was asking for her help on a problem I already knew the answer to. She knew I already knew the answer - but I was asking anyway. I just was. She said to me "Jessica, you have so much potential, I hope you allow yourself to become as great as you are."

I thought "great at hairstyles?!" No. I knew that was NOT it. (LOL) Oh I have it, I'm great at picking a colorful wardrobe. That I knew how to do well. BUT, she didn't say that. She thought I was great. Just me. She was great and thought I was great. I insulted her hair and she STILL thought I was great. She's the best person ever right?! (LOL)

Her words stuck with me. For some reason they affected me. I thought, I MUST be what she said I am. She wasn't my mom, she wasn't family, and she was a genius. She could do Calculus on the board, compute numbers in her head, and still know if we weren't paying attention. So to me she had to be RIGHT!

That day something inside me changed. I thought to myself, I CAN be great, but I had a dilemma. Being great interfered with my career as a hermit. I couldn't hide AND be great! I had to MATTER. I had to Be A Big Deal!!

So what did Michael Jackson sing? (singing) "I'm talking to the man in the mirror?"
(*Nodding*) I began talking to the girl in the mirror. Instead of STARING I would say (*point at "mirror"*) You Are A Big Deal!!

Every day I repeated this. I talked to the girl in the mirror. I would start my day off saying, say it with me, You Are A Big Deal. You Are A Big Deal. I was asking her, like Michael did, to "change her ways." I couldn't hide. I must be great. I must reach my full potential. Mrs. Preslar said it!!

I would go to bed and say to the girl in the mirror, say it with me, You Are A Big Deal. I began changing my clothes. I picked out cooler colors. Fitting clothes. I asked my mom to help me style my hair - and SHE DID!!! THANKS MOM!! (LOL)

I kept saying it, You Are A big Deal. I began working on loving me, CHANGING the messages I said to myself. That changed the way I perceived myself.

It changed the way I BELIEVED in MYSELF!!

When my day was bad and I felt no one understood me, I said, You Are A big Deal

When I made mistakes, felt guilty, and thought can I make things better for myself and right my wrong? I said, You Are A big Deal, you can do this!!

Then one day I looked in the mirror and guess what I said? I said I AM A BIG Deal!!!

(*More confident tone*) It became a part of me. I became a big deal to myself. Mrs. Preslar's words stuck with me that day and changed my life. They are one of the main reasons I can stand before you today.

When I was 16 I knew everything. I knew I couldn't be responsible for my own failure. 16 year-olds aren't big on responsibility, and 16 year-old me was not going to be responsible for that! Mrs. Preslar, (*pause*) she saw my greatness and she told me I wasn't ALLOWING myself to be great.

(*Stronger tone*) If I can do it, you CAN too. Talk to the person in the mirror. Ask that person to make a change. Tell yourself, YOU ARE A BIG DEAL.

That relationship you're struggling in? Tell yourself, YOU ARE A BIG DEAL.

That job where you feel you aren't getting the recognition you deserve? Tell yourself, YOU ARE A BIG DEAL.

Those times when you want to stay home and quit everything? Just quit life? Tell yourself, (*motion crowd to join in*) YOU ARE A BIG DEAL.

When that goal is taking longer to achieve and you think it isn't worth the hassle and energy anymore? Tell yourself, (*motion crowd to join in*) YOU ARE A BIG DEAL.

(*pause*) All those years ago in junior high I had it in me, what it took to be here today. The love, the energy, and the BELIEF. I still had it that day in high school with Mrs. Preslar. I still have it NOW.

(*Rising tone and volume, pointing*) You have it in you NOW. What it takes to be great. Now, AND tomorrow, AND 10 years from now.

Don't speak your insecurities, speak what you are to yourself. Say it with me: I. AM. A. BIG. DEAL!!!

You Are A Big Deal!

Thank YOU

2
SURROUNDED BY DARKNESS

***

Two a.m. the clock read. Amy has been sitting on the couch for hours staring at the clock. Her clothes smell of three-day-old pizza. She couldn't remember the last time she went to the bathroom. Was it before the last episode or three before that? Did she even have the urge to use the bathroom? She thought about going to work the next day, having missed four days already, but she did not feel like going in. She didn't want to see the many faces. Mr. Jameson was so demanding. Customers who were always impolite and demanding. The friends at work who wanted to share their life on breaks and wanted answers about her never-changing life, demanding. All she could think about work was it was too much. It was too demanding to shift from the couch and just move. She did not feel like moving much less showering. To turn on the water, to take off the comfy pajamas that have clothed her without demands for the last four days. To wash her hair in the shower. Oh to lift her arms. Just the thought of it made Amy feel more tired and finally sleepy. To sleep. Sleep has escaped her for the past week so she took one day off to rest and maybe sleep. Still no sleep and now no work. She scrolled through her phone at the missed calls and texts. "I'm okay," was her only reply so her mother would not call the police and place a missing person's report. She thought she should call Thomas back so he wouldn't worry but then he would ask questions and she didn't have the energy to give him answers and hear his replies. He meant well but it just all felt so... Demanding. There was no way to escape. The demands were everywhere. Exhausting and endless. She felt like she was unable to please anyone including herself. She was surrounded by darkness.

***

The darkness. Before you can begin the path to loving yourself, you must realize that you are doing the opposite. You are not loving yourself. Amy was trying to take care of her needs initially and then it became something else. Self-preservation. The dive into the darkness begins with self-preservation. The desire to protect yourself from someone or something that you believe is a threat either emotionally or physically. That can be as simple as draining your energy, as it has been with Amy, or it can be protecting yourself from outside forces that are threatening such as bullying, abandonment, rejection, abuse, etc. Somewhere it started on the outside and then you allowed it to move inward and you became surrounded by the darkness with no guide to get out. Let's talk about what ways in life we can move from self-preservation to hurting ourselves.

Withdrawal. Amy was in her home without friends or family. She was not returning calls or text messages. The very thought of having to engage with others made her feel weighed down and tired. Amy started withdrawing as a way to increase her energy by attempting to get more rest. Initially, this was probably a great idea. If you feel tired and need more rest, take it. Get some extra sleep and take care of you. When taking care of you moves into isolating yourself from everyone for extended periods of time, then it has become a problem. Amy had family and friends who loved her and were trying to reach out to her. You are never aware of who can help until you allow someone in. Amy was not loving herself by not talking to others. She was not taking care of herself by sitting at home in clothes that said she was giving up on everything. She was communicating just that to her mind and body. We are giving up on everything. She was ensuring the very thing she was trying to do, did not happen. Her body could not rest. Her mind could not rest. It wants to survive and Amy was not surviving this way. She was slowly sinking into a deep hole that she couldn't get herself out of. Withdrawal only leads one place. Loneliness.

Inactivation. You stop doing the things that keep your body moving forward. Work. Exercise. Eating. Drinking. The more immobile you are the more fatigued your body feels. The harder it is for you to get going again. Amy started by resting her body. This was good. Then she stopped going to work. She stopped showering. She stopped walking. She stopped being active. She was just being. The body is meant to do more than just "be." There is very little love in place when you are not taking care of your most important instrument. Your body. Not washing it. Not feeding it. Not giving it exercise even in minimal quantities like walking to the car or walking around at work. Shoot, walking around the place you live. The cycle of fatigue revs itself up when you do this and the tiredness needs more rest and more rest and then you are a stinky person with no energy to change your position. This is not self-love. This is not healthy.

Messages. Amy didn't express the messages to herself that were negative, but I'm sure we can think of some. I am never going to be good enough. I cannot get the raise I want. I have this and that flaw that keep me from getting the life I want. I will never reach these goals because I do not have XYZ. These messages do not help motivate us to move forward and work towards our best selves or our best lives. If you are not loving on yourself with words and messages you think or say about yourself, then how do we expect the light to overwhelm the darkness? When we think, say, and repeat negative messages about ourselves then we enlarge that dark hole. We validate the space it occupies and give it room to grow. Every time you say a negative message, or think it, you might as well say to the darkness, "I want you more than I want the great version of me." You start to believe those messages and it becomes harder to remember the positive things. It is then even harder to believe other people's positive statements about yourself.

Sabotage. Things are going great. That job is moving right along and you are excelling. The relationship you are in has been growing and things are headed right where you have been desiring. That goal you have worked toward is almost here. BAM! You suddenly do something that causes things to stall, halt, or go straight to the pits. Right before the end you do the very thing you know will ensure you never get what you actually desire. The very good will not happen. You undo all the steps you have taken forward. You sabotage yourself. The feelings of fear that something will happen and steal that goal away from you overwhelm you, and you act to cause the destruction yourself. You stop that promotion from happening at work. You detach in that relationship and slow the progression. You eat a large bowl of ice cream and two large slices of cake and prevent the scale from reflecting your hard work at the gym. You sabotage. In the sabotage the fear feelings are gone. You confirm those negative messages you have been saying to yourself by ensuring they come true. It's a cycle full of anxiety, hate, anger, sadness, and darkness.

Let's revisit Amy.

***

Finally, Amy thought moving from the chair. Standing in the middle of her living room, she contemplated what to do next. She picked up the phone, scrolled to Emily's name, and texted her.

"Hey… wanna do something today?"

"Sure… skipped work so free to hang all day."

"Ok. Come over."

Amy plopped back on the couch laying down facing sideways. She felt she took a step to do something to relieve her boredom. She thought about changing her clothes and decided there was no need to change for Emily. After all, she was coming over and they would just hang as usual.

Thump. Thump. Thump. Amy realized Emily was banging on the door. She got up lazily and walked slowly to the door.

"About time you open the door, lazy bones," said Emily as

she walked through the door quickly and made her way comfortably through the apartment.

"I was in the living room, I didn't hear you knocking at first, come on in."

"This place smells like horrible B.O.! Gosh Amy, what in the world?!"

Amy looked down in shame. Now wishing she didn't have on pajamas that had pizza stains on them, and she at least brushed her hair. "I have been trying to rest. I have been so tired lately."

"Tired or not Amy, this is horrible." Emily looked at Amy and her clothes. She looked away and walked over to sit on the couch. "Whatevs. What you watching on TV?" she asked, picking up the remote. "The remote's dead! Ugh… I can't.

"Amy, I'll come back another time. This place is horrible. You look like you smell, your hair's a mess, you have on your give-up clothes, and I'm just not feeling this today. I'll call you this weekend." Emily walks slowly through the house looking around shaking her head and then leaves.

Amy stands there watching the door. She falls to her knees and raises her hand to her face, wiping a tear from her eye. She felt drained. She moved to the couch and laid down taking a sigh. She thought this was going to be her life. She was going to be alone and in her house by herself because she couldn't get it together.

***

Attitudes. The way we think about things and the way we approach things (our attitude) both affect how we act. I like to think of attitude in expectancy. If you approach life with the expectancy of anger, negativity, or a nonchalant space, then that is what you reflect. You walk around angry, negative, or with an "I don't care" presentation. That presentation then affects your overall performance, your relationships, your job, and every interaction you have in life. Your attitude can stem from your mood, past experiences in life, and expectations due to history, fears and anxiety, etc. Amy had a "do not care" attitude and a "leave me alone" attitude. Emily reacted to her attitude and reflected it by leaving Amy alone to continue her position of not caring. Amy's attitude represented that she did not care about the things around her so why would someone else care more than she does. Amy may actually care more than what she allows others to see, but what she displays is that she is not caring and therefore she receives that from her friend.

Behaviors. This should be a "duh" moment but if it were, I would not be writing this. Negative behaviors are actions we take that affect our life in a negative way. I do things that hurt me, my life, or hurt others. There are so many forms of negative behavior that lie in the darkness. Poor behaviors attract other negative people into your life. There are some people who like doing these things and they will gravitate to others who are doing the same. Bad behavior also pushes the friends and family in your life who could pull you up, away. You will eventually not respect your actions and this increases your feelings of sadness, regret, anger, and darkness.

We have highlighted briefly some of the ways we move

from self-preservation to hurting ourselves. Awareness is the first step on this path. If you are unaware you are in the darkness, unaware that you are doing things yourself to remain in a place of sadness, anger, hurt, anxiousness, stagnation, and darkness, there can be no change. You can understand that you are experiencing these feelings. You can understand that this place is uncomfortable to you. You may even desire relief. Until you understand that YOU are doing things yourself to increase your position in the darkness or you are not doing anything to let the light in, things will remain the same.

This path begins in the mind so now is the time for an activity to get you thinking.

ACTIVITY 1:

Get a piece of paper and reflect. Take some time and think about your life. Are there ways you began trying to take care of yourself that turned into negative patterns? Did your life look better to you before, were you happier at another time?

Write down the times during the last two weeks when you felt angry, sad, anxious, or just in a dark space.

Next, write down what YOU did in that moment that either increased this feeling or what you did not do to remove it.

Finally, call three friends or family you trust to be honest with you. Not the friends or family that are always there to tell you everything you do is a great idea. We want the person that challenges you and you can count on to tell you that your breath smells or you have something in your teeth.

Ask each friend for their help. Get their opinion on the three things you are doing to hold yourself back in life. Write them down.

Do not argue or go against them. It's their opinion. You can ask for them to explain and give an example of when they have witnessed you doing it. Take notes.

Keep these. You will need them later when you are working the steps to loving yourself.

3
PAST FAILURES

***

Amy was running as fast as she could. She could hear her breathing in her head. Sounds of panting. She felt her heart beat fast and heavy in her chest. Almost so fast it stopped her breaths. She heard Thomas counting and she was leaning forward with anticipation to run. She couldn't let him win this time. He has been beating her in every race at Thanksgiving since he hit puberty and passed her in height and muscle mass. One. Two. Three! They take off running. She feels determined to win, physically tired, and happy she gets this time with her brother.

She smiled to herself sitting in her living room. She had not gone home for a visit at Thanksgiving in the last five years. Work, relationships, and just feeling ashamed that she quit college and was working as a secretary in a doctor's office kept her home. She wanted to be more. When did things change? She looked at the calendar. November 18th. Thanksgiving is approaching soon and she would love to see her family. Will they be mad that she hasn't returned their calls and texts? Are they disappointed in her? They say they are proud of her but they cannot be. She failed at what she set out to do. They had to feel as bad about her as she felt about herself. Walking into the kitchen, she stopped smiling and looked troubled. She suddenly felt the urge to lay down and take a nap.

***

There are many things in life that hold us back. Not excelling at something, quitting a goal, and trying but not completing things in life are some of the many things we call past failures. Anytime we are not successful at something it is called a failure. It is easy to move on from something that you excel at, or even move on from something that you were lukewarm about, but when you fail at something you were going one hundred percent with, it hurts. These are hard for some of us to move on from. We feel it deep in our soul and no matter what reason exists, we attempt to correct it in our minds or we attempt to punish ourselves even if we don't realize it.

Woulda-Coulda-Shoulda Tragic Thinking. Past failures happen to everyone. There are many successful people and the one thing they tell others is that they failed many times before they hit the jackpot. So why do some of us hold on tighter to the pain of failure than the others? It's all about perspective. When you look back at the failure that haunts you, I bet you are thinking of all the things that went wrong. What things were not in place. What you did not do that you could have. Who was not there. What you would do differently if you had the chance to change time and go back. Thinking like this does not help. This is what I like to call woulda-coulda-shoulda tragic thinking. This you can do all day. In everything, this a big yard of quicksand. You start with one question and it never ends. The more you question yourself and relive that moment, the more you sink into a hole of despair about you and your actions.

Notice how Amy not only thought this about herself, but she began to think that other people believed these things about her as well. They did not say anything about her past failings to her, but she believed that they had somehow entrusted her with the same amount of power she gave herself. None. The reality is this is all in her head. Amy's family nor friends have talked down to her or said she was a failure. This was all her at this time. This was all her feeling this way, and boy aren't we happy feelings aren't fact. They can feel that way but the great thing is they are NOT.

So, how do we stop giving past failures so much power over our thoughts and emotions? How do we regain control over our energy, mood, and motivation that is drained by woulda-coulda-shoulda tragic thinking??? We flip the coin. We start to think of the POSITIVES. What did I do right? A lot may have gone wrong but what went right? We learn from the mistakes. I may not have done this correctly, let's make a mental note to myself: *Self, don't do that again. Correct it by doing XYZ next time.* These things we correct in ourselves. Those successful people I was speaking of earlier? That's what they do, they correct themselves and move forward.

Shame. Past failures can also cause us to feel distress due to a perceived wrongful act or behavior that we turn on ourselves and we become the wrong thing. This is defined as shame. Shame leads to feelings of inadequacy, regret, unworthiness, and low self-esteem. These feelings caused by shame, whether valid or invalid, can cause a person to want to withdraw from others, or be alone with themselves to avoid feeling ashamed. Let's look at Amy.

Amy was so ashamed of herself for not completing college that she did not want to go home to see her family. She has not gone home. The shame she felt about not reaching the goal she set for herself she allowed to cause her to withdraw from her family. The very thought of what they could POSSIBLY be thinking about her caused her to be still and separate herself from the very people that love her most. This is anxiety. She is anxious about what they might feel about her, what they might say, or what she might feel when she is around them. The degree of shame she feels is so intense and negative, that she cannot believe they think anything else but that she is a failure as well. Anxiety is worrying about something that has not happened yet. Amy's family has not said these things to her, she just believes that they will or that they do think these things. Whether they do or not no one knows, but her perception is that they do and that perception has prevented her from experiencing life with her family.

How is shame lessened or even better removed completely? First, we start looking at what we did correctly. Then we begin to adjust. Adjust ourselves. When we feel that shame feeling trying to poop its nasty, hairy, gooey self out, we use positive self-talk. We say, "Hey NO, you are not correct. I am capable. I am a great person and deserve to keep moving forward and being great." When you feel like staying away from family and friends, because they are horrible psychics and know how bad you feel about yourself so they eagerly agree with you and feel the same way, (as if this really happens!) FIGHT IT. Go visit them anyway. Socialize. Receive the love, laughter, and joy you deserve. When your mind tells you that you don't, they won't, say to it, "You are wrong," and then attempt a perspective change. Tell yourself the very thing you do not think. Forgive yourself for that mistake you made and move forward. We will talk more about forgiveness later. Let's go visit Amy.

***

One, two, three, four stars. Amy counted as she laid in bed trying to fall asleep, attempting to distract her mind from replaying that day over and over in her head. The day she decided not to go to class for the first time. That day led to the next day not going and now she was laying across the bed thinking. *No falling stars*, Amy thought. She wished for a falling star so she could make a wish and have a chance at a do-over. She would go to class that day. Tired, hungover, and unprepared but she would be there. She would not restart the cycle that led to her quitting.

Amy thought of what her dorm mates were all doing now. She pulled her phone from under her pillow and started scrolling through Facebook. Carla- she looks happy, she is a teacher, she is doing great things. Zae- she just had a baby, she is a nurse, she is a big deal. Roxanne- she is an artist, she looks amazing, she is doing her thing. Me- I am a secretary, I look like crap and I hate my life. Tears filled her eyes and she threw her phone to the end of the bed and buried her face in the pillow.

Bonk. Bonk. Bonk. The alarm sounded. Amy stared at the clock. She didn't realize she fell asleep. She sat up in bed turning the sheets looking for her phone. "Got it!" Amy exclaimed and then she looked at it and saw her Facebook picture on the screen, remembering last night. She laid the phone down. "I HATE MY LIFE!" she yelled. She stood up angrily and marched to the shower.

***

Getting Stuck. Dwelling on past failures without actively attempting to push yourself forward leads to being stuck. When a person is stuck, they are constantly reliving the moment of failure. They are repetitively examining that time period, mistake, day, and choice over and over looking for a way to do it differently. The problem is they don't physically live in that moment anymore and cannot correct it in the past while living in the present. Therefore, they get stuck. Stuck in a loop emotionally and cognitively. They feel those feelings daily and they think the same thoughts over and over. It appears to others as if they can't move on or they are obsessive. They are trapped in a loop they have set for themselves to continue. You can give credit to your past failures, learn from them, AND still move forward.

ACTIVITY 2:

Here is a blog I wrote on the *Healing Acts* page called "A Mistake Can Be Your Greatest Achievement." Steps 1-5 apply to healing from past failures, BUT it also helps to ensure we don't get into the same emotional and cognitive place with current failures.

A Mistake Can Be Your Greatest Achievement

You are going along in life. Things are good, not perfect, but they are moving forward. You are working hard, preparing, checking yourself and you are seeing progress. Then one day, BOOM. You make a mistake. All of a sudden that progress either shifts backwards or it's at a standstill. Guess what??!! This can be the best thing to happen to you.

Here are 5 steps on turning a mistake into an achievement.

(1) Minimize damage. You probably thought I would say reflect and look here. NO. What you want to do immediately is harm reduction. Stop the consequences from rolling into a mountain. Take action first. If you can decrease the repercussions for you and others… .

Try your best. Give your BEST effort ladies and gentlemen. Don't give up.

(2) After you have minimized the damage, now sit. Look at what has happened and reflect. Do the who, what, when, where, and how. Own what you could control. Be honest with yourself about what you could not control. List these so you can see them.

(3) You know that serenity prayer. The part that goes… "God grant me the serenity to accept the things I cannot change; courage to change the things I can; and wisdom to know the difference." There is a reason this is so popular. LEARN.

LEARN. What can you change within yourself to ensure the mistake is not repeated? What can you change about your actions/behavior to ensure it doesn't happen again? Change those. The things you cannot change… ACCEPT!

It's crucial you accept what you cannot change. You learn your limitations. You do not want to be cycling in madness, trying to change something that is never possible with your effort, your wisdom, and your strength. We learn from limitations and strengths. We learn what we are capable of. Learn here.

(4) Forgive yourself. Mistakes happen ALL the time. Forgive yourself for this. You are human and you are not perfect. Let the anger, sadness, and fear go. You do this by completing steps 1-3. Then, reinforce to yourself that although this mistake was not wanted and did not feel great, things WILL get better. You are alive and this mistake doesn't change your worth or your value.

(5) Allow time. If you have completed the steps above, give time its turn in the process. You have minimized the damage. You have looked inside yourself and taken ownership of what you can. You have made changes where possible. You have learned as much as you can from this so it is not repeated. You have forgiven yourself and given yourself grace. There is nothing you can do now but move forward and allow time to show you… You have learned. This situation will come again and you will succeed at not making the same mistake. Achievement exists here. Not falling for the same struggle. Passing the test when it is presented again.

You are an achiever. A mistake does not mean you fail repeatedly or that you are not great. The reaction and steps you take when you make a mistake either hinders or fosters growth. In growth, we ACHIEVE!!

Walk yourself through the steps above. Take your time and truly work the principles.

4
EMOTIONAL PAIN

You are hurting. Someone did something to you and it's painful. You trusted someone and they betrayed you. You made a mistake and the people you thought supported you through everything, left. You feel isolated, alone, and lost.

So you try to keep it together. You go to school or work and try to just make it through each day. You hold it in and prevent any sign of weakness, so you feel strong. You believe you have everyone fooled. You feel as if they can see right through your charade but no one says a thing.

Time passes. Some days you don't feel the pain. You barely feel at all now. Some days you hurt but it's not as tangible as before. It's there but it's dull, nagging, and long lasting. Secretly, you want someone to notice. You want to be found out. You want someone to see your pain. You want someone to feel your pain.

Now, you are lashing out. You are sad and angry. You find yourself being short with your loved ones. You snap at random strangers. You decide to be alone more because you feel no one understands and you are irritable all the time.

You don't know how to break free. How to feel better. How to stop looking at yourself as if you are watching a movie. You want to feel connected again. You want to feel whole again.

Now… CRY PLEASE.

You start by crying. This may sound silly but it is key. Get to a place where you allow yourself to reflect on what happened and how you were hurt. Allow those emotions to come over you, and CRY.

Crying releases the physical effects from emotional build up.

You need to release the emotional buildup on the surface. The physical tension from trying to be strong and keeping things together. We begin here because the process of healing includes the physical as much as the mental.

You will soften. You will feel. The connection between mind and body is established fully. You start to feel like you again. It's the start of the journey.

With each tear you are closer to healing.

CRY. PLEASE!

The purpose of the CRY is the release. So many of us attempt to shoulder emotions and bottle them up within ourselves. The blog post above spoke about hurt, and the intense feeling of pain that results from it, because that is one of the most common ways we stop loving ourselves. When we are burdened with intense emotional pain, we often neglect our needs and our sense of importance. We suffer and we want it to go away but we are unaware of how to get that result.

Emotional pain is a way your body tells you, "Hey self! There's some crap we need to handle under the hood and it needs taken care of ASAP." That feeling of depression, sadness, worthlessness, and pure pain can tell you exactly what needs to be addressed if you sit with it.

Acceptance. Plenty of times we try to wear the mask or "fake it until we make it" as they say. We pretend to others AND ourselves that everything is fine. That we do not hurt as deeply as we do. That our blood has dried and we are healed when we are still bleeding deep inside with no end in sight. That's why we start with acceptance first. Accept that you are hurting. Allow yourself to feel the pain. To validate to yourself that this thing has happened and now…
I am hurt.
I ache.
I cry.
I am sad.
I am angry.
I am… changed.

Acceptance has to happen so you realize you need to do something to heal. To move forward. To help yourself NOT hurt.

Relinquish control. There are things you did and there are many you did not. Bad things happen to good people. It is not always your fault means it was not in your control. There are times when you just need to say, "Hey self, that was completely crappy that we just went through that and there was nothing now I could do to prevent it from happening." This seems to many like a victims statement and many perceive it as powerless, BUT it can be one of the most empowering things you say to yourself. You had no control over the bad thing that happened to you. It just happened. It just is.

Reflect and introspect. Take time to think about how you have changed because of this event and this pain. You have changed. Know that. YOU HAVE CHANGED. Take note of what you would like to incorporate in the future to not only survive, but come out a winner next time. Sometimes you cannot prevent a future event but you can prepare to be successful with the next challenge when it presents. Reflection and introspection aids that by you knowing what armor you have in stock and also what you need to acquire for yourself.

Ask for help. You have friends, family, coworkers, neighbors, counselors, Facebook friends, and random helpful strangers who you can turn to for help. Go to them to talk. You will be surprised how many of them are jumping at the chance to be there for you in any capacity. Go to the ones you know will listen to you and provide empathy and validation. Also, go to the ones who will challenge you to overcome that painful place and try to pull you up from the barrel. Some people will support you from above and some will support you and pull you up with them. Both serve purposes but we want more of the latter to rise and shine. Let's revisit Amy.

***

Amy stood there smelling the scent of lavender. She had always found the scent calming and sort of refreshing. She was watching the second hand on the clock in the lobby click slowly by, realizing she could hear it tick to a level where she could slightly feel the jerky movements it made. Her knee was starting to be in rhythm with the clock. She realized she felt really nervous waiting for Mr. Jameson to come out of his meeting. The door opened and a lady in a brown suit stepped out. Amy was holding her breath. Mr. Jameson gazed at her briefly then closed the door. She looked at the floor then back at his door. Should she leave? Will he come out and meet with her? Glancing around the room she wondered if anyone else could tell she was nervous. It made sense if they could, her knees were shaking and she was still breathing rather quickly. She looked up to hear Mr. Jameson, "Amy, come on in."

Amy rose sharply and pulled her jacket down to straighten her clothes. She followed Mr. Jameson into his office. They entered a room twice the size of her apartment. She noticed all the flowers. Lavender. She smiled and felt a bit calmer. Mr. Jameson couldn't be but so scary if he has lavender in his office. He gestured for her to sit.

In front of her was a large redwood desk, long and wide. There, Mr. Jameson sat behind it in a leather chair. "So, Amy. What brings you here today?"

Amy looked up. "I wanted to speak with you about returning to work."

Mr. Jameson nodded. "I see."

***

Meditate. Meditation is when you attempt to lessen the energy associated with negative emotions and channel positive energy, thereby increasing positive emotions. Basically, I am saying lets change the feeling of your presence. Your spirit. Your aura. The thing you radiate all day and night. Meditation is helpful because you can empty your brain. Get some of that junk out for a bit and feel relaxed and positive. Shifting your energy is important for how you approach life, tasks, people, and handle minute everyday struggles.

ACTIVITY 3:

Acceptance is so important that the activity for this section is all about ACCEPTANCE.

Acceptance may appear at first simple but is very complicated. There are parts of us that attempt to deny, reject or stall. Work these 4 steps to acceptance.

1) Let go of all belief that it's possible to stay in the emotional state you are in. You won't believe how hard your will tries to hold on; even when your mind says, "OK, I've let go." Start discarding things that will hold you back or make you desire to stay stuck. Let go of glue.

Distance yourself from friends and family that are negative with you or talk negatively about you. They don't have to agree but they do need to support you verbally, with their actions, and by allowing you to have positivity in your life.

2) Observe, rework, observe, rework. Observe yourself

and your behaviors daily. Are your actions supporting your change? Are they preparing you for the change? Are they somehow starting the parts of the process possible? Observe, then rework.

Rework. When you realize as we ALL do, that something we are doing is not helping, is holding us back, or is just hindering us from shifting our mindset, MOVE it.

Rework your behaviors. Rework. Rework. Rework. Until you have refined it enough that you are doing the best you can to not hinder your transition mentally or physically.

3) Plan. You know enough about the things that hold you back now to begin planning for mood elevation when you are down. Planning helps reduce our likelihood of going backwards or stalling, or just not progressing with the change.

What do we plan? We want to plan for FAILURE!! Bet you didn't see that coming. Yes. Plan for failure. Here we want to list signs, behaviors, and ways we know when we are going backwards or not adapting to the change well.

For example, if it's an ex-relationship that triggers you to feel sad. I know I get lonely at times so I may call my ex. I can foresee that calling my ex will be a behavior that will happen and cause me to stall or fail this mood change into positivity. So, I plan for this. I will place a block on my phone that makes it difficult to call or text my ex's number. If the problem is that the person will call me, I place their number in my spam folder so I receive no text or calls unless I go looking for them.

We plan for failure which helps further our success or adjustment.

4) Keep pushing forward. To truly accept change, you must stay committed to moving forward. That means when you feel scared, nervous, hesitant, or whatever emotion that prompts you want to sit still or turn around, you take that off the table.

Being stuck is NOT an option. You removed it as an option. Onward and forward. Be your own cheerleader. Encourage yourself. Remaining the same is NOT an option. I think I can. I think I can. I KNOW I can. You ARE a big deal.

If you do these steps, you are moving through full acceptance and are in a better place with your transition than most. Transitions can be anxiety provoking but they happen with or without your cooperation. It's better when we are an active participant.

You CAN do this! You ARE a big deal.

5
FORGIVENESS

Forgiveness is something that we all struggle with. Forgiving ourselves and forgiving others. Forgiveness is when we purposely decide to let go feelings of hurt, anger, resentment, or retaliation against someone else or ourselves, whether or not it was warranted or deserved. When we forgive we choose to let it go and move on. If we hold on to it, we feel it keeps us protected or powerful by not letting us forget, but in reality it makes us weaker and the very thing we are trying to have power over, has power over us.

The process of forgiveness sounds simpler than it is living it out. We can want to forgive someone but the pain prevents the release. I am going to talk forgiveness from a psychological perspective and a spiritual perspective.

Psychological- Here are some steps to forgiveness:

1) Forgiveness starts in your mind. Make a decision to forgive. You have to purposely think, *I am going to release this emotion I have for said person free.* Your emotions take longer to

catch up but the mental choice must be there first. Take holding on to the pain off the table. When you feel those negative emotions rising up, tell yourself, "Not now, I am over this. I am moving on."

2) Forgiveness requires your release. When we refuse to make a choice to forgive, we believe we are exerting power over the situation and the offender. The reality is, it controls your emotions and thoughts about it until you decide to take it back through forgiveness. Release the pain. Cry, scream, tell the person who hurt you what you felt and that you forgive them, or write a letter to them, or a pretend letter, and throw it away. Find a way to release it. You can be creative here.

This can appear difficult to figure out since you must figure out how to release the thing you are holding against yourself. A letter to yourself, crying, screaming, or even going to see a therapist to discuss what emotions you have against yourself to facilitate release are options.

3) Be truthful. Be honest with yourself about what happened and who's to blame. Don't take on more responsibility for the incident than you had in reality. We talked about woulda-coulda-shoulda tragic thinking. Don't do that here. You made a decision but that doesn't mean you are to blame for someone else's negative actions toward you. If you are to blame, take ownership of your actions and what led you to make the error.

4) Forgive yourself. Give yourself the ability to make mistakes. We all make decisions that sometimes lead to bad experiences. Ultimately, you just made a decision. You're hurt and your pain was caused by someone else taking

advantage of that, or the mistake you made was one bad thing of hopefully many good things you have done in contrast. By forgiving yourself, you give yourself permission to keep experiencing life to the fullest. You give yourself permission to be open and free to enter the next day without weights or baggage.

5) Finally, realize forgiveness is a process. It is not instantaneous. You do some things to help lessen the sting of experiences and the rest is lessened through time, life, and experiences.

Biblically and spiritually are one in the same for me. In the bible, forgiveness is the act of pardoning someone who has offended against you. So you let go the debt or retribution owed to you for their offense.

God showed us love and forgiveness first when He sent his son Jesus to cover us by Grace so that all our sin is forgiven and we may enter heaven. He even taught us in prayer to forgive others as He has forgiven us. The bible states, 'Forgive us our sins, for we also forgive everyone who sins against us.' (New International Version, Luke 11:4). The bible teaches us that in order to forgive we must come from a place of love. In 1 Corinthians 13:5 when they speak of love it is noted that, "it keeps no record of wrongs."

'Get rid of all bitterness, rage and anger, brawling and slander, along with every form of malice. Be kind and compassionate to one another, forgiving each other, just as in Christ God forgave you.' (Ephesians 4:31-32)

Spiritually, we know that we must release the wrong done to us from a place of love. God loved us enough to do it for us, and we must try to love ourselves enough to let go of debt we put on ourselves from wrongdoings and debt we place on others for things they have done to us.

Spiritual- Here are some steps to forgiveness:

1) Be GRACEful. I always tell my patients everyone deserves a measure of grace. We all ask that others give us grace or forgiveness at times, let's remind ourselves to do the same. ' ... for in the same way you judge others, you will be judged, and with the measure you use, it will be measured against you.' (Matthew 7:2). Our Father watches how we try to forgive and what eye we look at others through.

The eyes of love recognize we are all sinners and must acknowledge that about each other. I am not perfect AND you are not perfect. We are all perfectly, imperfect people who will need forgiveness from ourselves and from someone else. 'Indeed there is no one on earth who is righteous, no one who does what is right and never sins.' (Ecclesiastes 7:20).

2) Don't hold on to the pain for a long time. The longer you think about what someone did to you, or the longer you let the pain of what someone has done to you linger, it becomes that much harder to overcome yourself and let it go. When we hold something against ourselves for years, doesn't it become a part of you?

The bible teaches us to realize that the sooner we make the

choice to forgive, the better. 'Do not let the sun go down while you are angry, and do not give the devil a foothold.' (Ephesians 4:26-27). The devil wants to attack your mind. Think of it this way. The longer you hold on to it, the more power the devil has over that energy.

3) Forgiveness helps you spiritually and mentally. When we let go of that anger, resentment, and pain from hurt, our thoughts, emotions, and spirit are clear to do God's work and our work. When you accept that holding on to this will not protect you or allow you to get even with this person, you can begin to heal.

4) Focus on God's purpose for your life. God has a plan for every one of us. Channel your energy, focus, thoughts, and emotions into completing that, and God will take away the pain from anything else. 'Therefore, my brothers and sisters, make every effort to confirm your calling and election. For if you do these things, you will never stumble, and you will receive the rich welcome into the eternal kingdom of our Lord and Savior Jesus Christ.' (2 Peter 1:10-11).

Here is a prayer for forgiveness for yourself.

Have mercy on me, O God, according to your unfailing love; according to your great compassion blot out my transgressions.

Wash away all my iniquity and cleanse me from my sin. For I know my transgressions, and my sin is always before me.

Against you, you only, have I sinned and done what is evil

in your sight; so you are right in your verdict and justified when you judge.

Surely I was sinful at birth, sinful from the time my mother conceived me. Yet you desired faithfulness even in the womb; you taught me wisdom in that secret place.

Cleanse me with hyssop, and I will be clean; wash me, and I will be whiter than snow.

Let me hear joy and gladness; let the bones you have crushed rejoice. Hide your face from my sins and blot out all my iniquity.

Create in me a pure heart, O God, and renew a steadfast spirit within me. Do not cast me from your presence or take your Holy Spirit from me.

Restore to me the joy of your salvation and grant me a willing spirit, to sustain me. Then I will teach transgressors your ways, so that sinners will turn back to you.

Deliver me from the guilt of bloodshed, O God, you who are God my Savior, and my tongue will sing of your righteousness.

Open my lips, Lord, and my mouth will declare your praise. You do not delight in sacrifice, or I would bring it; you do not take pleasure in burnt offerings.

My sacrifice, O God, is a broken spirit; a broken and contrite heart you, God, will not despise.

May it please you to prosper Zion, to build up the walls

of Jerusalem. Then you will delight in the sacrifices of the righteous, in burnt offerings offered whole; then bulls will be offered on your altar.

(Psalm 51)

ACTIVITY 4:

On a piece of paper write down one person you need to forgive.

Write down how you feel about this person and be blunt about the feelings.

Write down how not forgiving this person has hurt you or is weighing you down.

Sit in a calm, quiet place where you cannot be disturbed.

Sit with your back against a chair or the wall, something firm.

Make sure your shoulders are relaxed and your legs are still.

Take deep breaths in through your mouth to a count of four and release through your nose to a to a count of four.

Do this three times and then stop. Close your eyes.

Say out loud, in a calm voice:

I forgive _____.

I know they hurt me by doing _____.

I know right now I feel _____ about _____ and it is hurting me more than anyone else.

I forgive _____ and by forgiving _____ I give myself back the power it took from me.

I release the feelings of _____ that have been with me since this happened.

These feelings have been holding me down by _____.

I want to feel happy, joyous, and excited about life and holding on to this pain is preventing that.

I can do this one moment at a time and one day at a time.

Do this as many times as you need to until one day you realize you no longer have to go into a calm place to feel calm about the situation.

Start with one person at a time. After you have forgiven one then move on to the next until you are free from the pain you are holding that others gave with their wrongs against you.

6
RESPECT

Loving yourself requires that you respect yourself. This may appear to be something that is self-explanatory, but too often we are doing things that scream, "We do not respect ourselves." The definition of self-respect we will use is below.

Self-respect: to think highly enough of oneself by showing consideration for their own rights, feelings, thoughts, and needs with actions and words.

There are several ways we can disrespect ourselves that communicate to us personally and to others that our regard for ourselves is lower than we deserve. First, let's revisit Amy.

***

She sat in the lobby watching the clock tick. Somehow it felt the hand on the clock was moving slower than it was before she entered Mr. Jameson's office. She made her plea. She admitted her feelings and mistakes to him. She looked up startled, hearing a door open. She looked back at her knees when she saw it was someone walking into the lobby. She felt the need to look back at the woman walking in the door. Her hair was long and auburn, flowing as if this was its normal routine. Black skirt and pink blouse, ironed with a flowery scent for the atmosphere. "I'm here for the interview," she told Nancy. Nancy shot a glance over to Amy. *Dang it, she's here for my job*, Amy thought. Looking down seeing her knees shaking more, she placed her hands on them in an attempt to slow them down. She did all she could.

"I really want to come back to work, I'm sorry for what I did and I promise I won't do it again."

"You left us with no word Amy. You didn't call in. You didn't give us any information. You just walked off the job."

"I know. I was just... I was just... To be honest Mr. Jameson, I was going through something. I was feeling really down about my life and I stopped doing everything... even at home. I'm ready for a change now. I want to come back to work. If you would please give me a chance I promise I won't do that ever again."

"I would like to Amy, but it doesn't set a good precedent. You can't understand the position I'm in. As of this week we started interviewing for your position. I think it's too late. I really wish I could take a chance on you again but you were the one that made the choice to not come back to work."

"I know. I thought you might say that. I have written a letter to explain some things to you I knew I could never say in words. If you would just please read it."

"I think it would take more than a letter."

"Please, just read it. That's all I ask," Amy passes the folded piece of paper to Mr. Jameson. "I'll let myself out."

"Well, wait in the lobby. I'll read it now. No sense in prolonging the inevitable."

"Yes, sir. Thank you for your time."

Amy thought back on the conversation as she watched her possible replacement sit in the chair in front of her. She looked down, as they almost met eyes, to not give away her nervousness. She shifted in her seat feeling uncomfortable. She fingered at her hair to straighten it.

"Amy. Mr. Jameson will see you now," Nancy stated.

Amy shot a glance over at the girl in front of her, standing promptly. She pulled her jacket down to straighten it and walked quickly through the lobby and into his office.

Both standing, Mr. Jameson handed the letter to Amy open. She folded it quickly and placed it in her purse.

"Thank you for your time, sir." She turned to walk away.

"I have one question, Amy.

"Why would you let such a small mistake in life possibly ruin the rest of your life?"

"Sir?"

"You quit college and then you did the same thing when you quit here. Do you not see that?"

"You have to finish what you start in life."

"I know. I'm trying to change things now, Mr. Jameson."

"It's a little late after you stopped coming to work, don't you think Amy?"

"I had to try."

"I think… I think I am going to let you come back to work."

Amy screams, "Oh, thank you, Mr. Jameson!"

"Thank me by continuing to do your job. Keep me in the loop next time, Amy. You are a great worker. I never had to worry about you until this happened and that is why I'm giving you a second chance."

"Thank you, Thank you!"

"You are welcome. Go tell Nancy to come in and I will have her get with you for scheduling you again."

"Thank you so much sir," Amy scurries towards the door without looking back.

***

Respect yourself with physical care.

Taking care of your body so it feels as good as it possibly can is one of the first ways you start respecting yourself. Your body needs adequate food, rest, exercise, water, and love. Start finding ways to prioritize taking care of you. So many of us will place our job, our families, or any other obligation over our own physical needs. In the end, everyone suffers. If you start to wear thin then your output suffers. When you start to take just a few minutes here and there to nurture yourself, you feel better. Your baseline for loving yourself is met.

This is the baseline. If the baseline can't be done then you need to stop here and put this book down. You aren't ready to start the path to loving yourself. You will never be a big deal to yourself and therefore you will not be a big deal to anyone else.

If you know you ARE a big deal and physical care is your baseline then here is a list of things to do daily:
Shower/bathe
Brush teeth
Hair maintenance
Eat three meals
Drink eight glasses of water
Take vitamins or medications
30 minutes of physical exercise or some relaxation exercise

That's your baseline. If you are not doing these things every day, then start today!! Think of anyone you can that you know neglects these things for themselves. NO matter the excuse you are aware that person is struggling somehow. Your brain picks up that this person is not loving themselves physically properly. If someone can think that about you, it's time to revamp some things. Start now.

Respect yourself with your words.

So many times we say things that exclaims we have poor respect for ourselves. When we say words to others that are negative about ourselves, our lives, and what we are doing, we are telling ourselves we are not of value. Here are some examples of negative messages we say about ourselves:

I will fail.
No one loves me.
I can't do anything right.
I will never have ____.
It's hard for me to____.
No matter what, I don't ____.
It never works out in my favor.
I am unattractive.
I will never get a better job.
This is just the life I will have.

I'm sure you can think of plenty more and ones that relate specifically to you. Regardless of what they are, they convey that we think negatively and expect negative outcomes. The other way we use our words to disrespect ourselves is by saying negative things to others. When I say negative things to others, I convey that it is acceptable for others to say those exact same things to me. If you curse others, talk bad about their appearance, or talk down to them, you invite these same negative messages from others.

When I was in college, I had a roommate who often called other women the b*tch word. There were times when things would get heated on campus with her and other females, and someone would call her that name. She would be LIVID. Of course, I'm standing there like that's not a big insult for her because she uses the word all the time, as a positive and negative. Well, one day she comes to me and said to me, after a fight with another girl in our hall, that no one ever calls her that word. I said to her I don't use it so they know its not okay to call me that word. She look BEWILDERED!

To me it was simple. If I don't use it when I am angry, or when I am not, then you know that is unacceptable for me. In college, with kids, that principle worked for me and throughout life it has continued to work for me. I'm sure someone has called me that somewhere and somehow BUT they don't know me and have never said it to me personally. I give the respect with my words I wish to receive.

Start using your words consciously. Speak positively to your coworkers, spouses, children, friends, and strangers. Begin to use encouraging words, and when you're mad either choose silence or refrain from being obscene, vulgar, and just plain negative.

Put out the respect you would like to receive, then you show with your words you ARE a big deal to yourself and others start to take on that same narrative.

Respect yourself with your relationships.

Relationships are one of life's most precious gifts. The bond between two people that brings joy, love, nurturing, and growth is priceless. Too often, people are faced with the difficulty of having one-sided relationships. You are there for others way more than they are there for you. You give your time, advice, money, and love freely without expectation, but when you need someone you are often left to uplift and elevate yourself.

Another way you respect yourself is by making sure your love quotient is met, and that means making sure your relationships are mutually beneficial. How do you change this?? How do you turn those one-sided relationships into mutually beneficial relationships?

1) Let your loved ones know you value them and why. Sometimes your family and friends believe they are just in your life to be in your life. They think this is it. Validate their existence, importance, and presence.

Telling someone, "I love talking to you because you are honest, caring, and have my best interests at heart," goes a long way.

2) Clarify expectations. Too often, neither party truly knows what their role is in the relationship. Tell your friend, partner, or loved one what you desire or expect from them.

A simple statement such as, "I would like you to help me

grow as a person by telling me when I'm wrong or being honest with me, even if you think I will be upset," helps your person:

   a) Feel comfortable performing that role.
   b) Understand what you need from them.
   c) Realize the type of relationship you desire.

3) Be a role model. Do what you desire and let it be known. If you give of your time because you find that important and desire it. Do it. Say it.

For example, you pick John up from work at 3 a.m. on a Saturday morning. John says, "Thank you, I appreciate it." You say, "No problem John. I know you would do it for me, too. We have that type of relationship. We support each other in these type of situations."

Simply put, you did it and you said it. It's important you give what you expect. It's a biblical principle. Sowing and reaping.

4) Validate and Encourage. Validate when your loved one does something you desire and like. Even if it's by accident. Tell them "I really liked when you did X, Y, and Z. I needed that. It made me feel A, B, and C."

People need to know they are doing things correctly or even that it was pleasant. That provides encouragement and fosters repetitive behavior. You want that.

5) Ask. Sometimes we don't receive because we haven't asked. People are not mind readers and have different backgrounds. Ask for help. Give them the chance to say

yes.

6) Finally, use discernment, prayer, and wisdom to increase better people in your life. Some we cannot choose, others we can. You don't have to allow everyone in your circle and you should not. Choose wisely.

It's great to give in relationships and I know every one of you reading this is a BIG giver. You focus on meeting the needs of the people around you and that's an amazing trait to have. Great character and a gold star for you, BUT you ARE a big deal too!!!

You ARE a big deal. You matter in your relationship. If you aren't making sure your needs are being met, and your special people believe you ARE a big deal to them, as much as you believe they are a big deal, you can end up passed over and feeling that you don't matter to others.

Respect yourself by being honest.

Honesty. It is very hard being honest with ourselves and others. Sometimes we think we have and are being honest, but we have suppressed the truth from ourselves so much that we actually believe what we have been telling ourselves. You have to be honest with yourself for any of the other parts to work. If you say to yourself you aren't hungry because you do not want to take time to make dinner, you neglect eating. You suffer in the end whether it's from overeating later or starving, but you could've been honest with yourself and said, "Hey I am hungry, but I don't want to cook." Getting take-out or phoning a friend could have been in the solution, but it was not because you weren't honest with yourself.

This is a simple example but a real one. Too often we tell ourselves lies to not do something, but we really want to do it. It's okay to be honest with yourself. Allow you to face YOU! If you are lazy, then you know what you need to change. If you have been too passive, if you are honest, you know this. When you lie to yourself you blame others for holding you back.

Being honest with yourself is so complicated that it takes several steps to increase this skill. Here are steps to become honest with yourself:

Journal. Some of you just freaked out at just the notion. No secret agent is going to come in your home looking for your journal. If you are paranoid to the point it is scary, technology has made it now that you can have a journal password protected on your phone or tablet. It's an app. All spouses, friends, and family should respect the need for a private journal. Okay, back to the point.

Journaling is a great exercise for you to start weaving through the crap in your mind. Yes, I said crap. You can freely write dumb things and smart things. Reread it and go, *OMG I'm not making sense here,* or, *Wow, that is not the truth.* Try this: Journal daily, writing about your life. Your life as much as you want to write. Be detailed and describe your inner thoughts, bad emotions, and fears. This is the juicy stuff. That is the purpose of the journal, to expose your mind and for this we want to expose your mind to... YOU!!

Challenge yourself. When you tell people things and when you are doing things, question yourself and DO NOT accept the first answer. Have a dialogue with yourself and ask, is this my real intention, thought, or feeling at the moment? You will shock yourself and realize some things are not. Does that mean you have to change it right then? NO! It does start you being more aware of yourself and why you do what you do.

Ask others. By now you probably realize I am a fan of incorporating the people in your life into your move upward to realizing you ARE a big deal. Ask other people if the things you believe about yourself are true. I have a friend currently that when we were becoming friends she was in complete denial about the type of person she was. One day she asked me why she did not have more friends. I replied with a question, "Do you want my honest answer?" She answered yes. I'm sure it was hard for her to hear. She was and is a true sweetheart but she was so rude to people. She did not like that feedback and now you would never guess that she used to be rude. It took her wanting to face herself. I had to face myself and YOU will have to face yourself. You need a mirror and the people in your life who can be objective, honest, and kind with their answers. Include them.

Decrease repetition. When you realize you have been dishonest with yourself or someone else, take action to decrease that next time. Actively take measures to make sure you take time to respond or just be honest. If you are decreasing the amount of lying you are doing to yourself and others, then what is the point of being honest? You can't be a big deal being an honest liar. These things cannot coexist together. I know you ARE a big deal, so I know you understand the need to decrease the lies you tell to yourself and others.

ACTIVITY 5:

Here are seven quotes about self-respect. Place them in your office, on your wallpaper on your computer or phone, and say them to yourself often until you truly believe them.

"If you want to be respected by other, the great thing is to respect yourself. Only by that, only by self-respect will you compel others to respect you." -Fyodor Dostoyevsky

"They cannot take away our self-respect if we do not give it to them." Mahatma Gandhi

"Self-respect is the root of discipline: The sense of dignity grows with the ability to say no to oneself." -Abraham Joshua Heschel

"I cannot conceive of a greater loss than the loss of one's self-respect." -Mahatma Gandhi

"There is only one real misfortune: to forfeit one's own good opinion of oneself. Lose your complacency, one betray your own self-contempt and the world will unhesitatingly endorse it." -Thomas Mann

"I cannot compromise my respect for your love. You can keep your love, I will keep my respect." -Amit Kalantri

"Never esteem anything as of advantage to you that will make you break your word or lose your self-respect." -Marcus Aurelius

7
THE GOLDEN RULE

Do unto others as you would have them do unto you. The Golden Rule. The principle belief that you put out what you want to receive. The roots of this rule come from the bible. In Matthew 7:12 (NIV) *"So in everything, do unto others what you would have them do to you, for this sums up the law and the prophets."* You may wonder why is this important in loving ourselves. The golden rule is important because if we can understand what it is to do unto others appropriately, then we know we have a knowledge base of how to love ourselves. It establishes values and standards.

Let's start with kindness. Kindness with the golden rule is acting as we would have others act towards us. You would assume that people know kindness is required in order to love someone. Sadly, when we look at relationships we see: angry parents, spiteful couples, nasty coworkers, shunning church members, and rude strangers. With that being said, kindness definitely needs to be highlighted.

Kindness is defined as the quality of being warm,

affectionate, gentle, caring, helpful, thoughtful, unselfish, benevolent, compassionate, neighborly, generous, tolerant, charitable, and empathic. To be kind. How do we show these traits?

Honestly, it's simple for some and hard for others. We ACT kind when we:
    smile
    make eye contact
    be polite
    offer help
    hold doors to buildings and elevators
    use someone's name when you know it
    listen with your ears and eyes
    be patient
    ask someone how they are doing
    share
    shake hands
    show concern
    speak in a welcoming tone

Finally, when with others put our troubles and emotions aside long enough to show genuine warmth. That moment may be the moment that changes everything for them AND for us.

Being kind to others changes lives. One interaction CAN make a huge difference for us just as much as for the other person.

Accounting for the perspective of others is important in living out the golden rule. It's too common in our society to hear or read about people bashing others for decisions, values, and/or mistakes they have made. Anyone can write a thesis full of their distaste, disdain, and disapproval of another. Yet there are few that strive to relate with or see the perspective of another, regardless of their value differences.

Factoring in another's perspective with the golden rule is treating another's right to have different values and beliefs as we would have others treat our right to have different values and beliefs. This can be difficult for us. We may want to keep different beliefs separate from ourselves, fearing the influence they may have on our own. I challenge us though. If our beliefs are strong and solid, learning what someone else believes and why that is important to them shouldn't cause us to waiver.

Here, we listen. We simply ask questions and actively listen. Active listening involves:

1) Listening to what the person is saying while waiting to respond

2) Responding with body language showing you're listening and questions related to what they're saying

3) Repeating a paraphrase of what you hear to clarify you're getting the meaning of what they're trying to relay to you

Listening, truly listening, increases understanding. Try to understand the who, what, when, where and/or how of what you are discussing or learning about a person. Often we have intolerance due to ignorance and listening reduces that.

Show gratitude or thankfulness. Showing others we're

thankful is hard for some of us. We over think it, or don't think at all. Regardless, it is important to show we are thankful, grateful, and appreciative in a manner that the receiving person understands. Being grateful with the golden rule is showing appreciation for others as we would have them show appreciation for us.

Here are a few ways to show we are thankful:
1) Say It!! There is power in words. A simple "Thank you for xyz" goes a long way. Don't text it, email it, or wait for the right moment. Pick up the phone or get them face to face and say "Thank You."

2) Give time back to them. Another way to show someone we're thankful is increasing the amount of time we make for them in our lives. An extra call, text, email, or Skype chat goes a long way. They notice, trust me.

3) Do something special for them in return. Unless this person is a stranger, we should know enough about them to do something special in return. It doesn't have to be as large as what they did, but it's a way to say Thank You.
   a. If it's a co-worker who likes coffee, get them one on a random day.
   b. For a parent, grab flowers or a trinket.
   c. Grab a friend their favorite dessert.
   d. The special part is it's something they like already and we're doing it to make them smile, to say Thank You.
4) Change some things. Sometimes the best way to say thank you is by changing what made us need help. Friends and family look for progress. They love us

and want to help, BUT what they love more is to see us RISE from the help.

5) Change and rise. Show them it was a step for us and that they helped pull us up.

6) Pay it forward. Help someone else. To empathize with others and become a helper is a priceless way to say Thank You. Someone helped us and now we help someone else. It makes us feel good and the person who helped us witnesses their help spread through us. Help someone who can't help themselves.

7) Tell the story. We don't have to use names but there is power in the testimony. The power is HOPE. Show others that there are people who care, sacrifice, and HELP. We give them hope by telling the story of when we needed help and it was provided. This says Thank You by way of others.

Finally, be cheerful going forth. When we have help in our corner JOY should follow. Don't walk around bitter, angry, upset and down. Rejoice that we have help. The problem may not be gone but there are fighters with us in the battle. That's enough to smile and be thankful for. People look for our spirit to rise. Show them their help is effective. Demonstrate we feel the help. Shift our attitude. Be joyful.

Let's revisit Amy.

***

Amy grabbed her phone from her purse excitedly.

"Hello?" Emily answered.

"He gave me my job back," Amy screamed. "I did what you said and it worked. He read the letter and decided to give me a second chance. Thank you so much Emily."

"That's amazing Amy. I'm so happy for you."

"You did this, thank you."

"It was all you girl. I'm just happy you've decided to fight for happiness now. I didn't like seeing you so down for the past few weeks."

"I didn't like it either, I just needed a push and you gave me that. Well you... and I was just tired of being that way over and over. You know?"

"I know."

"Have a meal with me tonight to celebrate?"

"Umm... only if we're going out and I'll pay!"

"It's a date, see you later! Love you my friend."

"I love you, too"

***

ACTIVITY 6:

This exercise is an external challenge with someone else.

This challenge is tricky because you must find a way to help the person without them knowing YOU are the one helping.

Pick a person, either someone you know or a stranger. It doesn't matter who the person is, but pick someone you know has a need you can meet.

Take your time and watch them. Sometimes what we think someone needs is actually a want, not a need.

Watch them and find ways to ask them questions. You must gain more information about them so you're aware of what they need.

After you have the information, prepare to help them anonymously.

Whether you are delivering something or setting up a service it must be anonymous. Nothing can trace back to you, packaging, service location, notes, nothing.

Once you have it all set up, do it! Put the plan in place.

Write about the experience.

Write about your thoughts and feelings throughout the entire process.

Come back to this in two weeks and see if you feel the same or if something has changed.

8
DARKNESS TO LIGHT

In chapter 2 we discussed ways we are surrounded by darkness. You have since begun walking The Path to Loving Yourself. We are starting to think to ourselves, you ARE a big deal. When we look in the mirror we know we are important, we matter and most importantly we have to show ourselves this. We are reducing the impact of past failures on our present and preventing them from hindering our future. We are finding ways to heal and let go of our emotional pain. Giving grace to ourselves and others through forgiveness has become paramount. We show ourselves respect, allowing others to pick up on it and respect us in kind. Treating others as we want to be treated is on a sticky somewhere in our environment.

We have done a lot already on this path to shine light into the darkness. The path to heal us from the inside. To feel, think and live as we desire and deserve. Let's revisit those concepts from chapter 2, making the light shine brighter and turning the darkness into light.

Withdrawal. I hope if we've learned one thing in this book it's that I believe we need each other. We need others and they need us. Withdrawing into ourselves and isolating from others gives power to darkness.

To prevent yourself from withdrawing you can:
Join a group at church, or a meet me in your community
Go to lunch with a friend at work
Invite a friend or sibling to dinner
Skype a friend for a chat
Go to the gym or park and be social
Participate in social clubs
Get involved in giving back
Complete work assignments, or homework, at a coffee house

There are so many ways we can include others at our level of comfort, involving one to a few people depending on what we need. The important thing is to start including others socially. Start slowly and incorporate them into our lives more regularly as our comfort increases.

Inactivation. Being idle for too long feeds the seed of darkness in the mind, encouraging it's growth. Think about how we feel down when we stop doing daily chores. Going to work we just feel worse. We need more sleep. We cannot get enough rest. It's like quicksand. All of a sudden we're in our grungy comfort clothes and look like we gave up on life. Stay active.

Ways to stay active:
Go to the gym
Go to church or your religious place
Go to work

Take a stroll around your neighborhood a few times a
week
Walk through the mall and window shop
Give yourself rewards at the end of the week for
tackling the weeks duties (work, school, etc.)
Try a new painting, drawing, or craft class
Ride a bike, go swimming, or play a sport
Go fishing

I could go on and on but I think we have the idea. Keep
moving unless you need rest. Rest is needed if you're active
but if you're not active then you haven't earned rest. Get
those feet and arms in gear. Do something that makes you
breathe a little harder. Our bodies and minds will thank us.

Messages. One of the main goals in this book is to drive
home a point. What we say to ourselves, both in our heads
and with our mouths, has power. I hope by now this is
redundant information for us. Negative messages are like
poison to our minds and souls, especially the messages we
accept as truth for ourselves. To combat negative messages
we want to use positive self-talk. Every time we have a
negative thought we counter it with two positive
statements.

For example, I think "Jessica, you can't do this book
thing. People will hate it." That's negative. Honestly, I
thought it. I countered that with "I can do anything I put
enough energy and research into. Everyone will not hate it,
it will help at least one person. That is the goal. To help."
We must fight ourselves. We must be the positive boxer in
our minds, fighting the low self- esteem boxer.

Sabotage. This one is harder to stop. Things are going well and as things get better in life, the pressure increases. Expectations from family, friends, and ourselves increase. Our brains, emotions, and bodies start feeling anxious and insecure, so we self-sabotage. We work to undo what we have worked so hard to put in place. Self-sabotage is hard to identify as it is often unconscious. We are unaware we are sabotaging. It's just really convenient when some life event or personal minor catastrophe happens and we can blame struggles on that. Sometimes we do this knowingly and that's when its chaotic. The relationship disasters we create to see if we can force the relationship to end because we're afraid of losing them. The promotion at work we pass on, stating negatives because we can't handle the competition.

The good news is we can work on preventing sabotage.

The ways to prevent personal sabotage and get out of your own way are:

1) Watch your moves and question yourself. Ask, "Why did I do that? Did I really not want it, or did I bow out because of the pressure?"

2) Realize you are not perfect and frankly, people don't expect you to be. Your success does not mean people in your life never expect you to fail at anything again. Understand that. Accept that of yourself as well.

3) Think about the people you let down when you self-sabotage. That relationship, that job loss, it doesn't just effect you, it effects someone else too. Try your best for both them and yourself.

4) Trying takes time. Be process oriented AND task oriented. Anything and everything is a process. Give yourself time. TIME. If you expect things to either change for the better overnight or tank right away you are ensuring sabotage. Give yourself time to watch things play out. It may or may not happen the way you want but the process can be enjoyable.

Attitude. Oh man, if I could give this to Wal-Mart cashiers I would. Just joking, but seriously how often have we come across a person attempting to ruin our day with their bad attitude? They're rude, unpleasant, and plain nasty to you for some reason that isn't your fault. Even in these situations we can control the expression of our feelings, so a bad attitude is never out of our control.

Here is how to combat being nasty or rude with others:
1) Introspection. Find out why you're doing what you're doing. Why're you being rude at work? At home? With your friends? Search yourself for the answer.

2) Change. We have a choice to change the situation and if we can't then we need to change our response to it. It's not okay to remain the same, so we change what we can. When we can't change anything we find a way to change our mood.

3) Find a guide. This can be real or fake. It can be a person on television, from a book or a person you know. You want to use the ways they handle situations, that you like and are positive, to guide

your response. Basically, copy someone else's responses until you find an authentic way to respond with a positive attitude yourself.

4) Finally, realize that you always have a choice. Think back to the Wal-Mart cashier that's negative. Her nasty attitude may be driven by something else. Try thinking about what in her life might make her treat others with such anger. We know that being rude is a choice, even while working as a cashier. We also know everyone is at a different place on the path. We can simply choose to engage minimally versus being outwardly nasty. We ALWAYS have a choice to behave the way we do. Make the right choice for the person you are with and yourself. The golden rule applies here.

Behaviors. There are things we do which hurt others and hurt ourselves. Control is key here. Practice self-control. Being angry doesn't mean we can hurt our spouse or children, physically or mentally. It isn't okay to destroy houses or other property either. It's okay to escape a situation by leaving for a while, then returning when calmer. We can choose to do something less damaging than hurting someone or something with our bodies or words. Even though we can be hurtful, we must choose not to.

This also applies to ourselves. Too often now, people hurt themselves when in distress. It isn't okay to harm yourself when you love yourself. If you don't love yourself enough not to harm yourself then it's time to seek outside help. Try letting someone else, preferably a professional, help you see why you're important and worth loving. The mechanisms in the mind that allow us to go this deep into self-harm are often a mixture of biology and life experiences, thus we need a professional to help us find our way out of the darkness. You can do that anonymously by calling a hotline or in person by going to a local community mental health center near you. Regardless, get help please!

Let's revisit Amy.

***

Amy arrived home smiling. She thought how great she felt having gone to Mr. Jameson and getting her job back. She scanned the apartment. Clothes were on the floor, dishes in the sink and on the counter, trash from two weeks ago still in the garbage, and enough empty bottles to fill a dumpster outside a bar.

She placed her purse on the counter and grabbed a note pad from the drawer. She began to write out a to-do list.

"Throw trash out, wash the dishes, wash and fold laundry, make up bed, spray and wipe counters, take bottles to recycle..... NEVER DO THIS AGAIN. I AM BETTR THAN THIS."

Feeling a tear drop, she moved slowly from the counter and she saw the letter she wrote hanging out her purse. She picked it up.

"Dear Mr. Jameson,
I am writing you this letter because I know I will not be able to find the words when I am in front of you to explain why I have failed you so miserably. I have been feeling down lately and rather ill. No, actually I have been dumping on myself. It is near the holidays and

every year this time it is hard for me to complete normal daily life. See I was once the prized child in my family. My parents thought I would become a great lawyer but instead I quit college. I quit not because it was too hard, not because I couldn't afford it, not because it was too my pressure, I quit just because. I was tired of being in school and working so I quit to work. It was a mistake. This time of year reminds me that I am not who I could have been and that my family should be disappointed in me. I am disappointed in myself. I could have done so much with my life. So for the last few weeks I have been laying in my house sulking. I have not been partying or having fun. I have been sulking, sir. My house looks a mess and smells awful. You would be terrified to see it and I would be mortified to have you see it.

My friends have refused to come back until I clean it because it is so awful. But last night I was laying on my couch and my friend Emily called me. She was talking to me about how I gave up on myself and the person I could have been I could still be. I honestly wanted her to shut up but she said something that made me think. She said I give up on everything because I give up on myself. As much as I hated to hear it, she was right. I do and I did. I gave up on myself after I quit college. I couldn't get past that decision and I allowed it to hold me back from everything I loved. I am ready now though to take my life back. I want to start changing that cycle and I want to be me again.

So, I am asking you to please give me a second chance. I know I do not deserve one but I am pleading for you to take a risk and let me prove to you and myself I can still be great at something. First, it will be your secretary. I will be the best secretary because now I am working on being me again. Not because of a job or because of college but because I can't give up on myself. Thank you for taking the time to read this letter. Amy."

Amy smiled at herself finishing the letter. She scanned the apartment again looking at the mess and she said "I am ready for the challenge, I won't give up again."

***

ACTIVITY 7:

Celebration Time.

Working on yourself is no easy task. It can be tiring and things feel like they are moving slowly.

Here is where we take time to celebrate the little milestones and accomplishments.

Take an hour and treat yourself to something you normally would not.

This can be:
Dessert
Outfit

Time alone to read
Dance party alone to your favorite song
A favorite meal
Friends night out

The idea is this must feel like a treat for you, whether its small or large. Take the time to celebrate how much you're accomplishing in this path. You're on it and you aren't quitting. Celebrate now. ☺

9
LOVING YOURSELF

There was a quote I read once by AVA that said, *"love yourself first, and you will always be in love."* I've mentioned several ways in this book we can increase the love we show ourselves. This chapter is focused on falling in love with you. How do we become involved enough with ourselves that we appreciate, adore and embrace all the parts of our self.

This is a comfortable love. Not a conceded, cocky, obnoxious, or arrogant love. This is an "I truly appreciate my good, my bad, and my ugly" love. An "If there isn't anyone else that takes care of me that's okay because I love me enough to make sure I take care of myself" kind of love.

We are each unique. Appreciate your uniqueness. There is no one else quite like you and that is a great thing. Being that we are unique, we don't need to compare ourselves to other people. We may set markers or have role models. We might strive to attain certain characteristics or attributes we admire in others. We don't say "if I were more like this person" or "if only I had the things that she/he has." We compare ourselves without realizing it. Today's society encourages comparisons. Who is the prettiest, has the best hair, makes the most money, is the most popular, wears the best makeup, drives the hottest car, etc. We live in a culture constantly telling us to compare ourselves and change our lives, telling us what we should or shouldn't have. Don't feed the need to "keep up" by comparing yourself.

Our own opinion on what to do with our lives, careers, homes, bodies, and overall happiness is the strongest one. What makes us happy should be the loudest sound in our ears. It can be tempting to change our needs and what we feel we deserve for others to make them happy. Compromising is good, but giving up our happiness is not.

We must always hear our own voice the loudest when considering our needs and thinking of what we deserve. We must speak up for ourselves and take make sure that we're happy even when we have to give a little.

Appreciate your accomplishments and failures. We live once. That's it. There are no do overs. Take time to write out the things you've accomplished in your lifetime. It can be things as simple as passing fourth grade, or complicated as fighting cancer. Our failures teach us lessons and we grow from them. That is how we appreciate our past instead of hiding from it. We are a product of those failures and we should appreciate the struggle.

Take time to list out the major failures. Think about what each struggle taught you about yourself. The way you were able to survive it because you survived it. The way we survive our struggles should cause us to love ourselves even more for our strength. We've made it through, even if by a shoe string. Go back over these and write out what you did and read it back to yourself. You'll be surprised at just how much you accomplished in "failure."

Make yourself a big deal to YOU. In relationships we prioritize spending time with other people and doing special things for them. We do this because we love them and we want to show them they're a big deal to us. We want to show them they're important to us and they matter to us. We must also do this with ourselves. Prioritize spending time alone with yourself. Use this time alone to take in the good and the bad. Sit with yourself and say "self we are doing x, y, z and boy do we need a, b, c." Get comfortable being alone and enjoying your own company. Take a run alone, or grab a small lunch by yourself. See how long it takes until you find peace being with yourself. Do it without distractions such as the phone, internet, or social media.

We must take time to care of ourselves. Do little things to show yourself you appreciate the things you are doing for your life. A massage, a pedicure, a salon day or just a gift for yourself. Do something to show yourself that you love you and that you are important. This may sound silly but it's very important. The time spent in our own company brings a peace. A peace that we can feel good, whether alone or with others. To fall in love with yourself is a hidden secret of people who are holistically successful. This is the place to find inner peace and pure love.

Write letters to ourselves is important. This could be in a journal. Take the time to tell yourself how think and feel about what is going on in your life right now. Tell yourself your desires. Be honest and let yourself know if you feel you're getting what you need and deserve. This raw honesty allows us to truly check in with ourselves and over time we'll grow to greatly appreciate it. Self- growth and self-awareness is at its highest when this is a staple. Open the lines of communication with yourself. You will appreciate it more than you realize.

ACTIVITY 8:

Get 4 pieces of paper. Do not look ahead.

Do each step before you look ahead at the rest of the activity.

Paper 1: Write down all the questions you would ask someone on a first date.

Paper 2: Write down all the questions you would ask someone if you were thinking about dating them in a serious relationship.

Paper 3: Write the questions you would ask someone if you were thinking about marrying this person.

Paper 4: Write down all the things you want to keep hidden from all three of these people. The things you don't want anyone but you to know.

Now take each paper and answer the questions yourself.

This is an exercise in knowing yourself. If you did this without cheating and you put forth great effort you asked the questions that were most important to you.

You asked the questions that matter for your interests and your heart to feel connected.

The things you want hidden were probably hard for you to write down but they came to the surface.

You should have had to face yourself here. To face you. A real chance to fall in love with yourself.

10
MOVING FORWARD

It's time to move forward on the Path to Loving Yourself. We've acknowledged the things we need to change, we've accepted that we're ready to change them, and we've prepared ourselves for the time it takes to make it happen. Now, how do we begin to move forward?

Roy T. Bennet said, *"You need to have faith in yourself. Be brave and take risks. You don't have to have it all figured out to move forward."* At this point, it's not all figured out but hopefully we're in a better place than we were before we started this book. The path does not end with this book and we need some keys to take with us daily while we're working the principles and moving forward from the darkness into the light where the love exists.

1) Have hope. Believe in yourself and your future. This may sound crazy but we cannot move forward while expecting or planning to fail. When we expect to fail we put less effort into things, our spirit is lower, and/or our energy is missing. With hope comes life, energy, and passion. We have to believe in positive results; believe we can affect

things for the better. We must hope it can be better.

2) Make a choice. Stick with it. Do you want to live, be happy, be married, get a new job, get over an illness, heal from a pain? We must decide on a goal along the path to loving ourselves, for every step. Try to be as specific as possible. For example, moving on from a bad relationship is a vague goal. A much better goal is: "In the next 8 months I will let go of my ex by throwing away keepsakes.""

With a specific goal the steps to moving forward begin to highlight themselves. The details of moving forward may look different for every one of us. Another example, a vague goal is to find a new job. A specific goal is to apply to at least 1 job which pays at least 10 dollars an hour every day. We can do this. Write the goal out. Look for ways to narrow the goal down from vague to specific.

3) Make decisions. Each of us needs to decide what we will and won't do. Make a choice. Choose to fight, live, heal, get another job, move on from a relationship, or fight past failures. Make a list of do's and don'ts. What holds you back? What are your vices? How long will you stop doing these things? Do you get a day off for relief and/or indulgence? What will you do daily, weekly and/or monthly to increase your positive energy, passion, and likelihood of success? Make a list for both. We are THE experts on ourselves. Be honest with YOURSELF about your needs and vices.

4) Take action. So simply put. MOVE!! Take some action. The goal, the do's and don'ts list; start putting them

into action. Start doing the steps it takes to reach the goal. Problems will arise. Don't procrastinate, stall or freeze. Tackle them with as few excuses as possible. This is the movement part. A plan without action is guaranteed to fail. You HAVE to act.

5) Finally, give a little grace. We must cut ourselves a little slack. There will be times when we make mistakes, get weak, have errors, or just fail. We can't get down on ourselves, letting it deplete our energy and weaken our spirits. Take a moment, regroup and learn from it, BUT keep moving forward. Keep trying. Every failure increases the chances of success next time. Learn from the mistake and let it go emotionally. We are human, not robots. Give yourself some GRACE!!

Do these 5 steps and you will see yourself moving forward on the Path to Loving Yourself. We are active participants through these steps. Remember, transition happens with or without our cooperation. It's better to be an active participant. You CAN do this!!

American theologian Reinhold Niebuhr came up with a prayer I believe is essential in the process of change in our lives. The Serenity Prayer.

The Serenity Prayer

God grant me the serenity
To accept the things I cannot change;
Courage to change the things I can;
And wisdom to know the difference.

Living one day at a time;
Enjoying one moment at a time;
Accepting hardships as the pathway to peace;
Taking, as He did, this sinful world
As it is, not as I would have it;
Trusting that He will make all things right
If I surrender to His Will;
So that I may be reasonably happy in this life
And supremely happy with Him
Forever and ever in the next.

Amen.

This prayer is so amazing because it highlights there are things in life we can't change and things we can. Additionally, this man knew enough about us to know shoot, sometime we won't know what we can and can't change. We may be fighting things we can't change and accepting things we can. Wisdom tells us which we can change and which we can't, preventing us from wasting energy in fruitless places. This leaves us energy for where it should be used.

It also keeps us mindful of patience. Life happens one moment at a time and one day at a time. That is all we can tackle at any given moment. If we focus on one moment at a time we increase our chances for success.

Giving in to a higher power. My higher power is God and I trust him completely to give me strength and joy when I am lacking the ability to find it within myself. He has not let me down yet. He was the one that led me down the Path to Loving myself. We all must defer to a higher power to fight the battle when we can't, to give us a joy that surpasses all earthly knowledge. You may not chose God but I did and I am forever happy with my decision.

ACTIVITY 9:

Get a corkboard and thumb tacks.

Acquire about 50 different magazines, from home and lifestyle to random ones you would see in the doctor's office.

Look through the magazines for things you think you want in your life.

If you want to be a doctor cut out a doctor.
If you want to feel loved cut out a heart, or the word love.

Get about 40 pictures related to what you want the Path to Loving Yourself to look like at the end.

Take the corkboard and creatively put the items on it with thumb tacks.

Put other things such as yarn, personal pictures, or mementos on the board as well.

This is now your **motivation board**.

The physical representation of your Path to Loving Yourself.

Have fun with it!!

Place it where you can see it every day. Reference it daily.

11
HEALING ACTS DR. K

This book has been brought to you by Healing Acts Dr. K. Healing Acts was created in 2014 to establish a medium for reaching people searching for someone to help them online who were fearful of talking to loved ones, friends, or professionals. It has since grown to a few thousand fans and received positive feedback from people it has helped. It is my goal to help people see lives reflect the love, joy, and success they desire and deserve.

Please go to the various online outlets and comment, like, and share with your friends and family:
www.healingactscoach.org
healingactsdrk (Facebook)
healing-acts.tumblr.com (Tumblr)
healing_acts (Twitter)

Here are a few blog posts from online I would like to share with you. Remember, the Path to Loving Yourself is unique to each and every one of us. I hope this book has helped you and can be a vehicle for change to you and someone you know.

Thank you for your support and generosity. Dr. Jessica Kerzner

When you notice you are seeking people out to agree with the choices you have made.... It's time to stop and make some changes. Finding YES friends doesn't mean you are doing things correctly... Trust the people who tell you the truth.. No matter how hard it is to hear. There you will find seeds for growth, change and the people that truly care about your future. ~Dr. K.

When you have been wanting something SO long and it feels like it's taking forever or you doubt it is going to happen.... Look hard at your options.. Have you exhausted them all? Have you done everything you can on your end to make it happen? Have you tried what you previously considered off limits for you? I know people who complain about not finding that perfect job but haven't tried but one option to locate possibilities. Look outside the box. Try new things and areas you might have considered off limits. Those areas might be where you find gold. See the unseen. ~Dr. K.

Healing Acts Communication Series: Part 1 cont. What is bad communication?

3) "Non-listening communication"- this is probably the easiest to identify from both perspectives. I will briefly go over it anyway. With this form of bad communication the person isn't listening. The person on the receiving end often repeats themselves, is not receiving eye contact,

experiences spaces in the conversation, and often wonders if the person is listening. If you are the person doing this, you are preoccupied, not giving your undivided attention, often feel lost in the conversation, need to be "caught up" on where things are, and you often hear people tell you "you don't listen."

4) "Knowledge focused communication"- this is when the person picks apart every little detail of what you are saying to correct the information versus listening to it as a whole. So they are correcting your grammar, names of places you mention, words you choose to use versus being more concerned with the message you are trying to relay. This isn't them trying to clarify details, this is when the most simple detail is fair game to be picked apart AND it does not add to the quality of the message. In fact, at the end of what you say, this person will need you to tell the story ALL over again to be able to get the message you were trying to convey originally.

On the flip side, the person could say they care less about details and want you to get to the point. These are details that matter AND are important to the message. Same thing then happens. The person on the receiving end has to repeat the information for them to understand.

5)"Non-engaged communication" -this you would think is the same as non-listening BUT it is not. Non-listeners are attempting to listen.. It's just done poorly. The non-engaged communicator acts disinterested. They act as if you are bothering them even if they agreed to talk. They don't ask questions, they don't make gestures like nodding their head in an attempt to communicate they are listening and they often rebuff others with their aloof presentation in conversations.

Most people who communicate poorly fall into one of the 5 forms of bad communication. Now that you know; what do you do?! How can you change it? That's Part 2 of this series... Steps to improve your communication style. ~ Dr. K.

Sometimes there is an event that happens in your life and you think you have hit rock bottom. You question all the decisions and actions you made that resulted in you being where you are. You feel as if noone can understand or help you because there is something unique about your situation and they can never compare. This is the time to Sulk, Reflect then ACT! ACT!

Sulk about the pain you feel and the horrible position you are in. Sulk means cry, pout and be miserable BUT do this for a short period of time. We are human, you are allowed to feel. Feel here.

Reflect on what were the poor choices you made and be honest about what you could and could NOT control. Accept responsibility for what you could have changed and accept that what you could not have controlled.... you simply could not have changed or impacted it.

ACT means change. Change what you can for the better. Whether it's a job, people, behaviors or your choices. You change what you CAN to improve your situation from here on out. ACT means we see the change you make. You behave differently.

Changing your life requires purposeful action. Heal on purpose. ~Dr. K.

"Once you decide there's no option to go back AND there's no way things can remain the same.... Your destiny begins!!!" ~Dr. K.

"The recipe to reach your destiny: Commit to a goal. Go after that goal with no excuses. Accept help along the way. Stay the course despite hurdles. " Dr. K.

It's when you are at your lowest point that you find unknown parts of yourself that cause you to Rise, Overcome, and become GREATER than you thought possible. When times are hard, don't quit trying.. search within and look for a way up! It exists just for you. You Can!!! ~Dr. K.

Sometimes we can feel stuck, unmotivated and unsure of our next move. We have a goal. We have a vision, yet we are unclear of the steps. Remember this is a feeling. Take a small step towards the goal. The motto "something is better than nothing" definitely applies here. Keep pressing forward!!! Stagnation NOT allowed!! Just keep moving.....~Dr. K.

Doubt can turn into discouragement quickly. Make the vision/dream a daily reminder of why you are working so hard, where you will be, and an ANTIDOTE for your doubts. You will get there. Be steadfast. Be resilient. Be GREAT! ~Dr. K.

You have committed to something. Everyday starting with that decision day moves you into the next level. To keep moving when it gets hard, when your faith feels weak, when your doubt yourself and when you feel you are your only cheerleader; prepare yourself a motivational song list, quote list and/or spiritual information list to strengthen your resolve. Here's one of my favorites. Dr. K

There comes a time in life you reach a pivotal crossroad in your life.... at this crossroad you have to face yourself. The mistakes you have made to get you there. The things you could have done but didn't. The weaknesses you are aware of that could prevent you from moving forward....... BUT.....

That's the time you need to remember how far you have come. The progress you have made. The steps that moved you forward... then focus on the promise. You have come a long way and you did that with ALL those mistakes and weaknesses...

The same you that began the journey... got through the middle of the journey AND will finish the journey!!! #pathtogreatness ~Dr. K!

A laugh a day can keep depression at bay. Laughter increases dopamine, which is your feel good neurotransmitter. A joke, song, movie, riddle or just daily silliness. Try to find something to make you laugh as often as possible. Laughter heals. Live. Laugh. Heal. ~Jess. K.

Just because you feel negative doesn't mean you have to act it out. The negativity cloud grows the more you feed it with anger, being unkind, withdrawing from others, being pessimistic and sulking in despair. Rise above your feelings and try to shift your mood by your actions. Shift yourself by being kind, looking at the positives, smiling, seeking friends and family for comfort, and exercise.

You are important. We need you to be the best version of YOU!! ~J.K

Don't give your power away. Trust yourself.

It can be hard after failing to trust in yourself and push forward in life. You can end the cycle of self- doubt, leaning on others to make decisions for you, and feeling incapable. Here are 7 steps to increase trust in yourself.

1) Stay in the present. Don't think about the past. Focus on the task at hand.

2) Take it slow. Pace yourself. Give yourself time to take in what needs to be accomplished and get it done.

3) Be active. Take action in your life. You are the leader not the watcher in your life. Make decisions. Take control. Don't allow others to control your life. You CAN do it.

4) Don't talk negatively to yourself. Be your own

cheerleader. Think and say positive things to yourself. Validate the steps you have taken from waking up to completing a task.

5) Nurture yourself. Eat healthy. Sleep enough hours. Dress to feel great. Treat yourself like you treat the people you care for and help daily.

6) When insecurities creep in, realize EVERYONE has them. The difference is everyone does not allow their insecurities to inhibit their actions. Push through. They are just thoughts and feelings....not FACT.

7) Keep getting on the horse. Always make an attempt. When everything inside you tells you to stop, hold back and you can't....... Take one more step. You CAN and WILL do it. Dr. K.

ABOUT THE AUTHOR

Dr. Jessica Kerzner is equipped with knowledge from academia and life. She has dedicated her life to helping others by volunteering, counseling individuals and families, crisis intervention, and giving talks. Led spiritually and by a passion/zest for people; she mentors personally and travels across the country helping others heal and reach their true potential.

Dr. Jessica Kerzner, Psy. D.

Jessica Kerzner CV

kerznerjessica@gmail.com

EDUCATION

- **Carlos Albizu University – Miami, FL**
- Psy.D. –Clinical Psychology

APA Accredited Program

Webster University- Charleston, SC
MA- Counseling Psychology
Marriage and Family Therapy

College of Charleston- Charleston, SC
B.S. –Psychology

CLINICAL EXPERIENCE

Healing Acts   08/14-
Present

Owner   Wichita, KS

- **Speaker and Coaching**: Conduct in person, via telephone or online; short and long-term individual life coaching to increase holistic adaptive functioning with adult clients. Completed with adult clients only.

- **Speaking:** Speak to groups from 10-200 people about various topics on mental health, empowerment and motivational themes. All ages.

Prairie View Inc
08/13- Present

Psychologist   Wichita, KS

- **Individual Therapy:** Conduct short and long-term individual, family therapy sessions with children/adolescents and adults with moderate to severe

94

psychopathology and families in outpatient and residential treatment settings.

- **Family Therapy:** Lead family therapy sessions with diverse families, including rural populations.

- **Group Therapy:** Lead adolescent and child process groups in a residential treatment setting once per week.

- **Crisis Intervention:** Provide assessment, intervention, treatment planning and referral for child, adolescent and adults at risk for suicide.

- **Assessment:** Administer neuropsychological, psychological and psycho-educational assessments for children/adolescents and adults. Score, interpret and complete a comprehensive report detailing clients' cognitive, achievement and personality functioning. Complete diagnostic assessments for children/adolescents and adults. Complete a thorough report recommending treatment recommendations.

- **Multi-Disciplinary Rounds**: Participate and present patient case information during case consultation meeting to coordinate services and develop treatment plans in an outpatient and residential setting.

- **Speaking:** Speak to groups from 10-60 people about various topics on mental health and trainings on assessments. All ages.

Wichita Collaborative Psychology Internship Program   08/13-08/14

Intern- Prairie View Inc. / Comcare Crisis Intervention Services Wichita, KS

- American Psychological Association fully accredited internship program.

- **Individual Therapy:** Conduct short and long-term individual therapy sessions with children and adolescents with moderate to severe psychopathology and families in outpatient and residential treatment settings.

- **Family Therapy:** Lead family therapy sessions with diverse families, including rural populations.

- **Group Therapy:** Lead adolescent and child process groups in a residential treatment setting once per week.

- **Crisis Intervention:** Provide assessment, intervention, treatment planning and referral for child, adolescent, adult and geriatric clients at risk for suicide. Provide emergency assessment on mobile location when the individual is at risk for psychiatric hospitalization and is unable to transport to a center. 8 hours a week.

- **Assessment:** Administer neuropsychological, psychological and psycho-educational assessments for children and adolescents. Score, interpret and complete a comprehensive report detailing clients' cognitive, achievement and personality functioning. Complete diagnostic assessments for children and adolescents. Complete a thorough report recommending treatment recommendations.

- **Multi-Disciplinary Rounds:** Participate and present patient case information during case consultation meeting to coordinate services and develop treatment plans in an outpatient and residential setting.

- **Supervision:** Receive two hours of individual supervision per week. Participate in two hours of clinical seminars per week emphasizing evidence-based treatments and current literature.

- **Supervisors: Katherine Minick, Ph.D., Elizabeth Guhman, Ph.D., Kathy Pearce, Ph.D., Susan Schatz, Ph.D.**

University of Miami, Miller School of Medicine 08/12-05/13

Extern –Neuropsychology Track
Miami, FL

- American Psychological Association fully accredited internship program.

- **Assessment:** Administer neuropsychological, psychological and psycho-educational assessments for children, adolescents, adults and elderly. Score, interpret and complete a comprehensive report detailing clients' neuropsychological, cognitive, achievement and personality functioning.

- **Consultation Liaison Services:** Complete neuropsychological consultations on the geriatric psychiatric unit and various medical floors.

- **Case Presentations:** Participate and present patient case information during team meetings two hours per week.

- **Medical Rounds:** Receive clinical seminars/presentations on current research and literature bi-monthly for 3 hrs a month.

- **Supervision:** Receive two hours of individual supervision per week. Participate in two hours of clinical seminars per week emphasizing case consultation and evidence-based treatment workshops.

- **Supervisors: Rosie Curiel, Psy.D., Rene Hernandez Cardenache, Psy.D., David Lowenstein, Ph.D**

Miami Children's Hospital
08/11-08/12

Extern -Child, Adolescent and Family Track
    Miami, FL

- American Psychological Association fully accredited internship program.

- **Individual Therapy:** Conduct short and long-term individual therapy sessions with culturally diverse children, adolescents and families in inpatient and outpatient treatment settings.

- **Family Therapy:** Lead family therapy sessions with diverse families, including international populations.

- **Group Therapy:** Co-lead adolescent and child process groups in an inpatient treatment setting. Co-led a Child Depression and Anxiety Group once per week. Development of the inpatient Child Relationship Group.

- **Assessment:** Administer psychological and psycho-educational assessments for children and adolescents. Score, interpret and complete a comprehensive report detailing clients' cognitive, achievement and personality functioning.

- **Consultation Liaison Services**: Complete behavioral medicine consultations on the Eating Disorder, medical floor. Provide bedside therapy and family therapy weekly.

- **Multi-Disciplinary Rounds**: Participate and present patient case information during team meetings on the Inpatient Psychiatry Unit and Eating Disorder medical floor five hours per week.

- **Supervision:** Receive one hour of individual supervision per week as well as three hours of group supervision per week. Participate in two hours of clinical seminars per week emphasizing case consultation and evidence-based treatment workshops.

- **Supervisors: Silvia Sommers, Psy.D., H. Michael Puhn, Ph.D., Moreno, Psy.D., Gilda Janet P. Rosen, Psy.D.**

Health Psychology Group of South Florida
01/11-10/11

Extern   Miami, FL

- **Individual Therapy:** Conduct short and long-term individual therapy sessions with culturally diverse adolescents and adults in hemodialysis and outpatient treatment settings.

- **Assessment:** Administer psychological, psycho-educational, neuropsychological and vocational rehabilitation assessments for adolescents and adults with mental retardation, spinal cord injury, trauma, and learning disabilities. Score, interpret and complete a comprehensive report detailing clients' cognitive, achievement, personality functioning and recommendations for treatment.

- **Consultation Liaison Services:** Complete behavioral medicine consultations on the Oncology and Cardiology medical floors in hospital settings. Provide bedside therapy as needed.

- **Case Presentations:** Participate and present patient case information during team meetings three hours per week.

- **Supervision:** Receive three hours of individual supervision per week as well as two hours of group supervision per week. Participate in two hours of clinical seminars per week emphasizing case consultation and instrument instruction workshops.

- **Supervisors: Roberto Sanchez, Psy.D., Linnette Castillo, Psy.D.**

H.A.P.P.Y Grant, Hialeah Miami-Lakes High/Carlos Albizu University 08/10-06/11

Extern   Miami, FL

- **Individual Therapy:** Conduct short individual therapy sessions with at-risk adolescents in a school setting.

- **Group Therapy:** Lead adolescent process groups in a school treatment setting once per week. Development of the Adolescent Trauma Group which utilizes a Trauma Focused CBT theoretical model.

- **Assessment:** Administer psychological and psycho-educational measure to adolescents in a school setting.

- **Supervision:** Receive two hours of individual supervision per week as well as one hour of group supervision per week.

- **Supervisor: Laura Alfonso, Ph.D.**

Neuro-Connections
01/10-01/11

Extern   Boca-Raton/Coral
Gables, FL

- **Individual Therapy:** Conduct short and long-term individual therapy sessions with geriatric patients with dementia in assisted living treatment settings.

- **Assessment:** Administer neuropsychological assessments for adults and geriatric patients with head traumas, and dementia in assisted living, outpatient treatment and residential settings. Score, interpret and complete a comprehensive report detailing clients' cognitive, achievement, personality functioning and recommendations for treatment.

- **Rehabilitation**: Complete computer assisted cognitive rehabilitation with patients diagnosed with traumatic brain injuries in assisted living and outpatient treatment settings.
- **Case Presentations:** Participate and present patient case information during team meetings two hours per week.
- **Supervision:** Receive four hours of individual supervision per week as well as one hour of group supervision per week. Participate in two hours of clinical seminars bi-weekly emphasizing case consultation and instrument administration and scoring workshops.
- **Supervisor: Melissa Becher, Psy.D.**

Goodman Psychology Center
08/09-01/10

Extern   Miami, FL

- Association of Psychology Postdoctoral and Internship accredited internship program.
- **Individual Therapy:** Conduct short and long-term individual therapy sessions with child, adolescents and adults in an outpatient treatment setting.
- **Assessment:** Administer comprehensive clinical intakes in an outpatient treatment setting.
- **Supervision:** Receive one hour of individual supervision per week as well as one hours of group supervision per week. Participate in two hours of clinical seminars per month emphasizing evidence based treatment workshops.
- **Supervisors: Ted Cunliffe, Ph.D, Ana M. Pi, Ph.D.**

ADDITIONAL CLINICAL EXPERIENCE

Dorchester Children's Center
10/07-04/09

Extern
Dorchester, SC

- National Child Alliance accredited program.

- **Individual Therapy:** Conduct short and long-term individual therapy sessions with children and adolescent victims of physical and/or sexual abuse using a Trauma Focused CBT theoretical model.

- **Family Therapy:** Lead family therapy sessions with victim families using Bowen Systems and Trauma Focused CBT theoretical models.

- **Group Therapy:** Co-lead parenting skills training groups utilizing Positive Parenting model in an outpatient treatment setting.

- **Assessment:** Administer trauma and psychological assessments for children and adolescents. Score, interpret and complete a comprehensive report detailing client's emotional functioning.

- **Forensic Services:** Complete forensic interviews of alleged child and adolescent victims of sexual and/or physical abuse using the Cornerstone research based protocol. Interpret and complete a comprehensive report detailing client's abuse for participating outside agencies. Participate as an expert witness during trial. Provide witness preparation as needed.

- **Liaison Services:** Complete trauma consultations for the school and police system.

- **Multi-Disciplinary Meetings:** Participate and present patient case information during team meetings three hours per week.

- **Supervision:** Receive two hours of individual supervision per week as well as two hours of group supervision per week. Participate in two hours of clinical seminars per week emphasizing case consultation and evidence-based treatment workshops.

- **Supervisors: Kay Miller, Ph.D, Jennifer Bunch, M.A.**

CERTIFICATIONS/TRAININGS

- Victim Service Provider, Office of Victim Services Education and Certification (OVSEC), VSP Number 01-0097, January 1, 2009
- Forensic Interviewer, Finding Words South Carolina, American Prosecutors Research Institute, 2008
- The Jason Foundation, "Awareness and Prevention of Youth Suicide" (February 13, 2009)
- Stewards of Children/Darkness to Light, Sexual Abuse Prevention Training (August 8, 2008)
- Victims with Disabilities: The Forensic Interview (June 10, 2008)
- Dealing with Difficult People (May 2, 2008)
- Mini-Conference of PTSD: "The Trauma Connection" (April 28, 2008)
- Finding Words South Carolina, American Prosecutors Research Institute (July 28, 2008-July 1, 2008)
- South Carolina Professional Society on the Abuse of Children- Colloquium (April 17-18, 2008)
- Failure to Thrive
- Assessing Sexual Abuse in the Context of Pediatric Condition Falsification and Parental
- Custody Issues
- Typology of Persons Who Sexually Offend Against Children
- Working with the Non-Offending Caregiver-Protection Clarification
- Gang Violence Prevention
- Girl Gangs: The Rise of Girls and Gang Life
- How to be an Effective Witness
- The Interface between Mental Health & the Law - A Judge's Perspective (March 7, 2008)
- Cooperative Parenting Skills Training
- Suicide Assessment and Intervention
- Parent Child Interaction Treatment
- Conscious Discipline Parent Skills Training
- Assessing and Treating Children with Mood and Behavior Disorders
- Assessing and Treating Trauma and PTSD

Made in the USA
Middletown, DE
16 February 2022

61323737R00068